Georgia Weekly Planner

With Complete Alignment to the Georgia QCC Objectives

Grade 1

Math ADVANTAGE

W9-CFS-861

ISBN 0-15-321588-7

1 2 3 4 5 6 7 8 9 10 179 2003 2002 2001 2000

Harcourt Brace & Company

Orlando • Atlanta • Austin • Boston • San Francisco • Chicago • Dallas • New York • Toronto • London

www.harcourtschool.com

Getting Ready for Grade 1

PLANNING GUIDE

Introducing the Chapter p. 1   **School-Home Connection** p. 2

OBJECTIVE	VOCABULARY	RESOURCES	GEORGIA QCC OBJECTIVES
GETTING READY 1 **2 DAYS** **One-to-One Correspondence** pp. 3–4 Objective To use one-to-one correspondence to compare equal groups	same number	■ Problem Solving, ■ Reteach, ■ Practice, ■ Enrichment Worksheets GR 1	**QCC 1.30** Recognizes equivalent and nonequivalent sets using one-to-one correspondence.
GETTING READY 2 **1 DAY** **More and Fewer** pp. 5–6 Objective To use one-to-one correspondence to compare unequal groups	more, fewer	■ Problem Solving, ■ Reteach, ■ Practice, ■ Enrichment Worksheets GR 2	**QCC 1.30** Recognizes equivalent and nonequivalent sets using one-to-one correspondence.
GETTING READY 3 **1 DAY** **Numbers Through 5** pp. 7–8 Objective To model and label groups of objects for numbers 0 through 5	zero, one, two, three, four, five	■ Problem Solving, ■ Reteach, ■ Practice, ■ Enrichment Worksheets GR 3	**QCC 1.20** Selects the numeral that names a group of objects and matches a group of objects with the appropriate numeral for a given set. **QCC 1.21** Counts by ones, fives, and tens to 100 and by twos to 20. Counts backwards from 20. **QCC 1.24** Recognizes, writes, and orally names numerals 0 through 100.
GETTING READY 4 **1 DAY** **Numbers Through 9** pp. 9–10 Objective To model and label groups of objects for numbers 6 through 9	six, seven, eight, nine	■ Problem Solving, ■ Reteach, ■ Practice, ■ Enrichment Worksheets GR 4	**QCC 1.20** Selects the numeral that names a group of objects and matches a group of objects with the appropriate numeral for a given set. **QCC 1.21** Counts by ones, fives, and tens to 100 and by twos to 20. Counts backwards from 20. **QCC 1.24** Recognizes, writes, and orally names numerals 0 through 100.
GETTING READY 5 **1 DAY** **Ten** pp. 11–12 Objective To model and label groups of 10	ten	■ Problem Solving, ■ Reteach, ■ Practice, ■ Enrichment Worksheets GR 4	**QCC 1.20** Selects the numeral that names a group of objects and matches a group of objects with the appropriate numeral for a given set. **QCC 1.21** Counts by ones, fives, and tens to 100 and by twos to 20. Counts backwards from 20. **QCC 1.24** Recognizes, writes, and orally names numerals 0 through 100.

OBJECTIVE	VOCABULARY	RESOURCES	GEORGIA QCC OBJECTIVES
GETTING READY 6 **1 DAY** **Greater Than** pp. 13–14 **Objective** To identify which of two numbers is greater	greater than	■ Problem Solving, ■ Reteach, ■ Practice, ■ Enrichment Worksheets GR 6	**QCC 1.20** Selects the numeral that names a group of objects and matches a group of objects with the appropriate numeral for a given set. **QCC 1.21** Counts by ones, fives, and tens to 100 and by twos to 20. Counts backwards from 20. **QCC 1.28** Identifies numerical relations of numbers 0 through 100 and sequences of numbers in ascending order. **QCC 1.30** Recognizes equivalent and nonequivalent sets using one-to-one correspondence.
GETTING READY 7 **1 DAY** **Less Than** pp. 15–16 **Objective** To identify which of two numbers is less	less than	■ Problem Solving, ■ Reteach, ■ Practice, ■ Enrichment Worksheets GR 7	**QCC 1.20** Selects the numeral that names a group of objects and matches a group of objects with the appropriate numeral for a given set. **QCC 1.21** Counts by ones, fives, and tens to 100 and by twos to 20. Counts backwards from 20. **QCC 1.28** Identifies numerical relations of numbers 0 through 100 and sequences of numbers in ascending order. **QCC 1.30** Recognizes equivalent and nonequivalent sets using one-to-one correspondence.
GETTING READY 8 **1 DAY** **Order Through 10** pp. 17–18 **Objective** To order numbers to 10		■ Problem Solving, ■ Reteach, ■ Practice, ■ Enrichment Worksheets GR 8	**QCC 1.20** Selects the numeral that names a group of objects and matches a group of objects with the appropriate numeral for a given set. **QCC 1.21** Counts by ones, fives, and tens to 100 and by twos to 20. Counts backwards from 20. **QCC 1.28** Identifies numerical relations of numbers 0 through 100 and sequences of numbers in ascending order.
GETTING READY 9 **1 DAY** **Ordinal Numbers** pp. 19–20 **Objective** To identify ordinal positions to fifth	first, second, third, fourth, fifth	■ Problem Solving, ■ Reteach, ■ Practice, ■ Enrichment Worksheets GR 9	**QCC 1.26** Uses ordinal numbers first through tenth to indicate position.

CHAPTER ASSESSMENT **Chapter GR Review/Test** p. 21–22

Chapter 1 Understanding Addition

BIG IDEA
Addition is the process of joining two groups, and it names the whole when the parts are known.

PLANNING GUIDE

Introducing the Chapter p. 23   **School-Home Connection** p. 24

OBJECTIVE	VOCABULARY	RESOURCES	GEORGIA QCC OBJECTIVES
LESSON 1.1 **2 DAYS** **Modeling Addition Story Problems** pp. 25A–26A Objective To model real-life addition problems	in all	■ Problem Solving, ■ Reteach,■ Practice, ■ Enrichment Worksheets 1.1 ◉ **Carnival Countdown •** *Bubble Band,* p. 26A ▱ Transparencies Problem of the Day 1 Spiral Review 1	**QCC 1.36** Solves one- and two-step word problems. **QCC 1.44** Relates addition and subtraction to words, pictures, and concrete models.
LESSON 1.2 **2 DAYS** **Adding 1** pp. 27A–28A Objective To use pictures to represent adding 1	sum plus equals addition sentence in all	■ Problem Solving, ■ Reteach, ■ Practice, ■ Enrichment Worksheets 1.2 ▱ Transparencies Problem of the Day 1 Spiral Review 1	**QCC 1.38** Recalls addition facts and related subtraction facts presented vertically and horizontally. **QCC 1.45** Determines addition and subtraction facts up to 18 using various strategies.
LESSON 1.3 **2 DAYS** **Adding 2** pp. 29A–30A Objective To use pictures to represent adding 2 and to write the sums	in all sum plus equals	■ Problem Solving, ■ Reteach, ■ Practice, ■ Enrichment Worksheets 1.3 ▱ Transparencies Problem of the Day 1 Spiral Review 2	**QCC 1.20** Selects the numeral that names a group of objects and matches a group of objects with the appropriate numeral for a given set. **QCC 1.38** Recalls addition facts and related subtraction facts presented vertically and horizontally. **QCC 1.45** Determines addition and subtraction facts up to 18 using various strategies.
LESSON 1.4 **2 DAYS** **Using Pictures to Add** pp. 31A–32A Objective To use pictures to describe addition situations and find the sums	in all sum plus equals addition sentence	■ Problem Solving, ■ Reteach, ■ Practice, ■ Enrichment Worksheets 1.4 ▱ Transparencies Problem of the Day 1 Spiral Review 2	**QCC 1.38** Recalls addition facts and related subtraction facts presented vertically and horizontally. **QCC 1.41** Uses appropriate mathematical symbols $(+, -, =)$. **QCC 1.44** Relates addition and subtraction to words, pictures, and concrete models. **QCC 1.45** Determines addition and subtraction facts up to 18 using various strategies.
LESSON 1.5 **2 DAYS** **Problem-Solving Strategy: Write Addition Sentences** pp. 33A–34A Objective To solve problems by writing addition sentences	in all sum plus equals addition sentence	■ Reading Strategy: Use Picture Clues, ■ Reteach, ■ Practice, ■ Enrichment Worksheets 1.5 Problem-Solving Think Along, TR p. R113 ▱ Transparencies Problem of the Day 1 Spiral Review 3	**QCC 1.36** Solves one- and two-step word problems. **QCC 1.44** Relates addition and subtraction to words, pictures, and concrete models.

CHAPTER ASSESSMENT **Chapter 1 Review/Test p. 35–36**

Chapter 2 — Understanding Subtraction

BIG IDEA
Subtraction is the process of separating from a whole or comparing two quantities.

PLANNING GUIDE

Introducing the Chapter p. 37   **School-Home Connection** p. 38

OBJECTIVE	VOCABULARY	RESOURCES	GEORGIA QCC OBJECTIVES
LESSON 2.1 **2 DAYS** **Modeling Subtraction Story Problems** pp. 39A–40A Objective To model subtraction problems	are left	■ Problem Solving, ■ Reteach, ■ Practice, ■ Enrichment Worksheets 2.1 ◉ **Carnival Countdown** • *Bubble Band,* p. 40A ▨ Transparencies Problem of the Day 2 Spiral Review 4	**QCC 1.44** Relates addition and subtraction to words, pictures, and concrete models.
LESSON 2.2 **2 DAYS** **Subtracting 1** pp. 41A–42A Objective To use pictures to identify how many are left when subtracting 1	minus are left	■ Problem Solving, ■ Reteach, ■ Practice, ■ Enrichment Worksheets 2.2 ▨ Transparencies Problem of the Day 2 Spiral Review 4	**QCC 1.38** Recalls addition facts and related subtraction facts presented vertically and horizontally. **QCC 1.45** Determines addition and subtraction facts up to 18 using various strategies.
LESSON 2.3 **2 DAYS** **Subtracting 2** pp. 43A–44A Objective To use pictures to identify how many are left when subtracting 2	difference are left	■ Problem Solving, ■ Reteach, ■ Practice, ■ Enrichment Worksheets 2.3 ◉ **Zoo Zillions** • *Annie's Jungle Trail,* p. 44A ▨ Transparencies Problem of the Day 2 Spiral Review 5	**QCC 1.38** Recalls addition facts and related subtraction facts presented vertically and horizontally. **QCC 1.44** Relates addition and subtraction to words, pictures, and concrete models. **QCC 1.45** Determines addition and subtraction facts up to 18 using various strategies.
LESSON 2.4 **2 DAYS** **Writing Subtraction Sentences** pp. 45A–46A Objective To write subtraction sentences	subtraction sentence difference	■ Problem Solving, ■ Reteach, ■ Practice, ■ Enrichment Worksheets 2.4 ▨ Transparencies Problem of the Day 2 Spiral Review 5	**QCC 1.41** Uses appropriate mathematical symbols (+, −, =). **QCC 1.44** Relates addition and subtraction to words, pictures, and concrete models.
LESSON 2.5 **2 DAYS** **Problem-Solving Strategy: Make a Model** pp. 47A–48A Objective To use the *make a model* strategy to solve addition and subtraction story problems		■ Reading Strategy • Use Word Clues, ■ Reteach, ■ Practice, ■ Enrichment Worksheets 2.5 Problem-Solving Think Along, TR p. R113 ▨ Transparencies Spiral Review 6	**QCC 1.36** Solves one- and two-step word problems. **QCC 1.44** Relates addition and subtraction to words, pictures, and concrete models.

CHAPTER ASSESSMENT   Chapter 2 Review/Test p. 49–50

CHECKPOINT
Chapters 1–2 Math Fun p. 51, Technology p. 52
Chapters 1–2 Take-Home Book pp. 52A–52B, Review/Test pp. 53–54
Chapters 1–2 Performance Assessment p. 55
Chapters 1–2 Cumulative Review p. 56

Chapter 3 | Addition Combinations

BIG IDEA
Thinking strategies can relate known facts to unknown facts.

PLANNING GUIDE

Introducing the Chapter p. 57   **School-Home Connection** p. 58

OBJECTIVE	VOCABULARY	RESOURCES	GEORGIA QCC OBJECTIVES
LESSON 3.1 **1 DAY** **Order Property** pp. 59A–60A Objective To explore the Order Property using *order*	order sum	■ Problem Solving, ■ Reteach, ■ Practice, ■ Enrichment Worksheets 3.1 ▫ Transparencies Problem of the Day 3 Spiral Review 7	**QCC 1.42** Uses concrete objects to explore the commutative property of addition. **QCC 1.45** Determines addition and subtraction facts up to 18 using various strategies.
LESSON 3.2 **1 DAY** **Addition Combinations** pp. 61A–62A Objective To identify combinations for sums through 8		■ Problem Solving, ■ Reteach, ■ Practice, ■ Enrichment Worksheets 3.2 ▫ Transparencies Problem of the Day 3 Spiral Review 7	**QCC 1.25** Recognizes different names for whole numbers through 20. **QCC 1.38** Recalls addition facts and related subtraction facts presented vertically and horizontally.
LESSON 3.3 **1 DAY** **More Addition Combinations** pp. 63A–64A Objective To identify combinations for sums through 10		■ Problem Solving, ■ Reteach, ■ Practice, ■ Enrichment Worksheets 3.3 ◉ **Carnival Countdown** • *Snap Clowns,* p. 64A ▫ Transparencies Problem of the Day 3 Spiral Review 8	**QCC 1.25** Recognizes different names for whole numbers through 20. **QCC 1.38** Recalls addition facts and related subtraction facts presented vertically and horizontally.
LESSON 3.4 **1 DAY** **Horizontal and Vertical Addition** pp. 65A–66A Objective To write addition sentences horizontally and vertically	addition sentence	■ Problem Solving, ■ Reteach, ■ Practice, ■ Enrichment Worksheets 3.4 ▫ Transparencies Problem of the Day 3 Spiral Review 8	**QCC 1.38** Recalls addition facts and related subtraction facts presented vertically and horizontally. **QCC 1.41** Uses appropriate mathematical symbols (+, −, =).
LESSON 3.5 **1 DAY** **Problem-Solving Strategy: Make a Model** pp. 67A–68A Objective To use the strategy *make a model* to solve story problems about money to 10¢		■ Reading Strategy • Use Word Clues, ■ Reteach, ■ Practice, ■ Enrichment Worksheets 2.5 Problem-Solving Think Along, TR p. R113 ▫ Transparencies Spiral Review 6	**QCC 1.13** Determines the value of a set of coins up to $0.50. **QCC 1.36** Solves one- and two-step word problems.

CHAPTER ASSESSMENT   Chapter 3 Review/Test p. 69–70

Chapter 4 Addition Facts to 10

BIG IDEA
Thinking strategies can relate known facts to unknown facts.

PLANNING GUIDE

Introducing the Chapter p. 71   School-Home Connection p. 72

OBJECTIVE	VOCABULARY	RESOURCES	GEORGIA QCC OBJECTIVES
LESSON 4.1 **2 DAYS** **Counting On 1 and 2** pp. 73A–74A **Objective** To use counting on 1 and 2 to find sums to 10	count on	■ Problem Solving, ■ Reteach, ■ Practice, ■ Enrichment Worksheets 4.1 ⊙ Carnival Countdown • *Snap Clowns*, p. 74A ▢ Transparencies Problem of the Day 4 Spiral Review 10	**QCC 1.38** Recalls addition facts and related subtraction facts presented vertically and horizontally. **QCC 1.45** Determines addition and subtraction facts up to 18 using various strategies.
LESSON 4.2 **2 DAYS** **Counting On 3** pp. 75A–76A **Objective** To use counting on 3 to find sums to 10	count on	■ Problem Solving, ■ Reteach, ■ Practice, ■ Enrichment Worksheets 4.2 ▢ Transparencies Problem of the Day 4 Spiral Review 10	**QCC 1.38** Recalls addition facts and related subtraction facts presented vertically and horizontally. **QCC 1.45** Determines addition and subtraction facts up to 18 using various strategies.
LESSON 4.3 **2 DAYS** **Doubles** pp. 77A–78A **Objective** To use doubles to find sums to 10	doubles	■ Problem Solving, ■ Reteach, ■ Practice, ■ Enrichment Worksheets 4.3 ▢ Transparencies Problem of the Day 4 Spiral Review 11	**QCC 1.38** Recalls addition facts and related subtraction facts presented vertically and horizontally. **QCC 1.44** Relates addition and subtraction to words, pictures, and concrete models. **QCC 1.45** Determines addition and subtraction facts up to 18 using various strategies.
LESSON 4.4 **2 DAYS** **Addition Facts Practice** pp. 79A–80A **Objective** To practice addition facts to 10	doubles sum	■ Problem Solving, ■ Reteach, ■ Practice, ■ Enrichment Worksheets 4.4 ▢ Transparencies Problem of the Day 4 Spiral Review 11	**QCC 1.38** Recalls addition facts and related subtraction facts presented vertically and horizontally. **QCC 1.45** Determines addition and subtraction facts up to 18 using various strategies.
LESSON 4.5 **2 DAYS** **Problem-Solving Strategy: Draw a Picture** pp. 81A–82A **Objective** To use the problem-solving strategy *draw a picture* to solve problems		■ Reading Strategy • Word Clues, ■ Reteach, ■ Practice, ■ Enrichment Worksheets 4.5 Problem-Solving Think Along, TR p. R113 ▢ Transparency Spiral Review 12	**QCC 1.36** Solves one- and two-step word problems. **QCC 1.41** Uses appropriate mathematical symbols $(+, -, =)$. **QCC 1.44** Relates addition and subtraction to words, pictures, and concrete models.

CHAPTER ASSESSMENT Chapter 4 Review/Test p. 83–84

Chapter 5

Subtraction Combinations

BIG IDEA

Subtraction names the unknown part when the whole and one part are given.

PLANNING GUIDE

Introducing the Chapter p. 85   **School-Home Connection** p. 86

OBJECTIVE	VOCABULARY	RESOURCES	GEORGIA QCC OBJECTIVES
LESSON 5.1 **1 DAY** **Subtraction Combinations** pp. 87A–88A Objective To model subtraction combinations for numbers through 8 and to complete the subtraction sentences	subtraction sentence, addition combinations, subtraction combinations	■ Problem Solving, ■ Reteach, ■ Practice, ■ Enrichment Worksheets 5.1 ● Carnival Countdown • *Snap Clowns,* p. 88A ▨ Transparencies Problem of the Day 5 Spiral Review 13	**QCC 1.38** Recalls addition facts and related subtraction facts presented vertically and horizontally.
LESSON 5.2 **1 DAY** **More Subtraction Combinations** pp. 89A–90A Objective To model subtraction combinations for 9 and 10 and to complete the subtraction sentences	subtract, subtraction combinations, subtraction sentence	■ Problem Solving, ■ Reteach, ■ Practice, ■ Enrichment Worksheets 5.2 ▨ Transparencies Problem of the Day 5 Spiral Review 13	**QCC 1.38** Recalls addition facts and related subtraction facts presented vertically and horizontally.
LESSON 5.3 **1 DAY** **Vertical Subtraction** pp. 91A–92A Objective To write subtraction sentences horizontally and vertically	subtraction combinations, subtraction sentence	■ Problem Solving, ■ Reteach, ■ Practice, ■ Enrichment Worksheets 5.3 ● Carnival Countdown • *Snap Clowns,* p. 92A ▨ Transparencies Problem of the Day 5 Spiral Review 14	**QCC 1.38** Recalls addition facts and related subtraction facts presented vertically and horizontally. **QCC 1.41** Uses appropriate mathematical symbols $(+, -, =)$.
LESSON 5.4 **1 DAY** **Fact Families** pp. 93A–94A Objective To model fact families and to write the sums and differences	fact family	■ Problem Solving, ■ Reteach, ■ Practice, ■ Enrichment Worksheets 5.4 ▨ Transparencies Problem of the Day 5 Spiral Review 14	**QCC 1.38** Recalls addition facts and related subtraction facts presented vertically and horizontally. **QCC 1.41** Uses appropriate mathematical symbols $(+, -, =)$.
LESSON 5.5 **1 DAY** **Subtracting to Compare** pp. 95A–96A Objective To model comparative subtraction and to complete the subtraction sentences	compare match	■ Problem Solving, ■ Reteach, ■ Practice, ■ Enrichment Worksheets 5.5 ▨ Transparencies Problem of the Day 5 Spiral Review 15	**QCC 1.38** Recalls addition facts and related subtraction facts presented vertically and horizontally.

CHAPTER ASSESSMENT   Chapter 5 Review/Test p. 97–98

Chapter 6 Subtraction Facts to 10

BIG IDEA
Subtraction describes the process of subtracting from a whole.

PLANNING GUIDE

Introducing the Chapter p. 99   **School-Home Connection** p. 100

OBJECTIVE	VOCABULARY	RESOURCES	GEORGIA QCC OBJECTIVES
LESSON 6.1 **2 DAYS** **Counting Back 1 and 2** pp. 101A–102A **Objective** To count back 1 and 2 to subtract from 10 or less	count back number line	■ Problem Solving, ■ Reteach, ■ Practice, ■ Enrichment Worksheets 6.1 💿 **Zoo Zillions** • *Number Line Express,* p. 102A ▢ Transparencies Problem of the Day 6 Spiral Review 16	**QCC 1.38** Recalls addition facts and related subtraction facts presented vertically and horizontally. **QCC 1.45** Determines addition and subtraction facts up to 18 using various strategies.
LESSON 6.2 **2 DAYS** **Counting Back 3** pp. 103A–104A **Objective** To count back 3 to subtract from 10 or less	number line count back	■ Problem Solving, ■ Reteach, ■ Practice, ■ Enrichment Worksheets 6.2 ▢ Transparencies Problem of the Day 6 Spiral Review 16	**QCC 1.38** Recalls addition facts and related subtraction facts presented vertically and horizontally. **QCC 1.45** Determines addition and subtraction facts up to 18 using various strategies.
LESSON 6.3 **2 DAYS** **Subtracting Zero** pp. 105A–106A **Objective** To subtract zero or all from a number and find the difference	zero	■ Problem Solving, ■ Reteach, ■ Practice, ■ Enrichment Worksheets 6.3 💿 **Zoo Zillions** • *Number Line Express,* p.106A ▢ Transparencies Problem of the Day 6 Spiral Review 17	**QCC 1.38** Recalls addition facts and related subtraction facts presented vertically and horizontally. **QCC 1.43** Explores the Property of Zero in addition and subtraction. **QCC 1.45** Determines addition and subtraction facts up to 18 using various strategies.
LESSON 6.4 **2 DAYS** **Facts Practice** pp. 107A–108A **Objective** To practice adding and subtracting 1, 2, and 3 to find sums and differences of 10 or less	count on count back	■ Problem Solving, ■ Reteach, ■ Practice, ■ Enrichment Worksheets 6.4 ▢ Transparencies Problem of the Day 6 Spiral Review 17	**QCC 1.38** Recalls addition facts and related subtraction facts presented vertically and horizontally. **QCC 1.43** Explores the Property of Zero in addition and subtraction. **QCC 1.45** Determines addition and subtraction facts up to 18 using various strategies.
LESSON 6.5 **2 DAYS** **Problem-Solving Strategy: Draw a Picture** pp. 109A–110A **Objective** To use the problem-solving strategy *draw a picture* to solve problems		■ Reading Strategy • Use Word Clues and Pictures, ■ Reteach, ■ Practice, ■ Enrichment Worksheets 6.5 Problem-Solving Think Along, TR p. R113 ▢ Transparency Spiral Review 18	**QCC 1.36** Solves one- and two-step word problems.

CHAPTER ASSESSMENT	Chapter 6 Review/Test p. 111–112
CHECKPOINT	**Chapters 3–6** Math Fun p. 113, Technology p. 114 **Chapters 3–6** Take-Home Book pp. 114A–114B, Review/Test pp. 115–116 **Chapters 3–6** Performance Assessment p. 117 **Chapters 1–6** Cumulative Review p. 118

Chapter 7 Solid Figures

BIG IDEA
Geometric figures in two and three-dimensions can be described, identified, compared, classified, transformed, constructed, and measured.

PLANNING GUIDE

Introducing the Chapter p. 119   **School-Home Connection** p. 120

OBJECTIVE	VOCABULARY	RESOURCES	GEORGIA QCC OBJECTIVES
LESSON 7.1 **1 DAY** **Solid Figures** pp. 121A–122A **Objective** To identify cones, spheres, and rectangular prisms and to relate them to real-life objects; to use spatial sense to identify solids from different views	rectangular prism sphere cone	■ Problem Solving, ■ Reteach, ■ Practice, ■ Enrichment Worksheets 7.1 ● Zoo Zillions • 3D Gallery, p. 122A Transparencies Problem of the Day 7 Spiral Review 19	**QCC 1.4** Identifies spheres, cubes, and cones. **QCC 1.33** Organizes elements of sets according to characteristics such as use, size, and shape.
LESSON 7.2 **1 DAY** **More Solid Figures** pp. 123A–124A **Objective** To identify cylinders, cubes, and pyramids and relate them to real-life objects; to use spatial sense to identify solids from different views	cylinder pyramid cube solid figures	■ Problem Solving, ■ Reteach, ■ Practice, ■ Enrichment Worksheets 7.2 Transparencies Problem of the Day 7 Spiral Review 19	**QCC 1.4** Identifies spheres, cubes, and cones. **QCC 1.33** Organizes elements of sets according to characteristics such as use, size, and shape. **QCC 1.45** Determines addition and subtraction facts up to 18 using various strategies.
LESSON 7.3 **1 DAY** **Sorting Solid Figures** pp. 125A–126A **Objective** To sort and classify solid figures by properties (stacking, sliding, rolling)	stack roll slide cone sphere rectangular prism, cube cylinder pyramid	■ Problem Solving, ■ Reteach, ■ Practice, ■ Enrichment Worksheets 7.3 ● Zoo Zillions • 3D Gallery, p. 126A Transparencies Problem of the Day 7 Spiral Review 20	**QCC 1.29** Selects elements belonging to or not belonging to a given set. **QCC 1.32** Sequences numbers and points on a number line and determines missing numerals (0 through 20).
LESSON 7.4 **1 DAY** **More Sorting Solid Figures** pp. 127A–128A **Objective** To sort and classify solid figures by the number of faces	face rectangular prism sphere, cone cylinder pyramid cube	■ Problem Solving, ■ Reteach, ■ Practice, ■ Enrichment Worksheets 7.4 Transparencies Problem of the Day 7 Spiral Review 20	**QCC 1.29** Selects elements belonging to or not belonging to a given set.
LESSON 7.5 **1 DAY** **Problem-Solving Strategy: Make a Model** pp. 129A–130A **Objective** To use the problem-solving strategy *make a model* to build cube structures	cone cube cylinder pyramid rectangular prism sphere	■ Reading Strategy: Use Picture Clues ■ Reteach, ■ Practice, ■ Enrichment Worksheets 7.5 Problem-Solving Think Along, TR p. R113 Transparency Spiral Review 21	**QCC 1.7** Identifies the shapes that can be put together to make a given shape.

CHAPTER ASSESSMENT Chapter 7 Review/Test p. 131–132

BIG IDEA

Geometric figures in two and three dimensions can be described, identified, compared, classified, transformed, constructed, and measured.

PLANNING GUIDE

Introducing the Chapter p. 133   **School-Home Connection** p. 134

OBJECTIVE	VOCABULARY	RESOURCES	GEORGIA QCC OBJECTIVES
LESSON 8.1 **1 DAY** **Plane Figures** pp. 135A–136A **Objective** To identify plane figures as faces of solid figures	circle square triangle rectangle face	■ Problem Solving, ■ Reteach, ■ Practice, ■ Enrichment Worksheets 8.1 ▢ Transparencies Problem of the Day 8 Spiral Review 22	**QCC 1.3** Identifies circles, squares, triangles, ovals, diamonds, and rectangles in various orientations/positions.
LESSON 8.2 **1 DAY** **Sorting Plane Figures** pp. 137A–138A **Objective** To sort and describe plane figures by the number of sides and corners	side corner rectangle square triangle	■ Problem Solving, ■ Reteach, ■ Practice, ■ Enrichment Worksheets 8.2 ◉ **Carnival Countdown •** *Pattern Block Roundup,* p.138A ▢ Transparencies Problem of the Day 8 Spiral Review 22	**QCC 1.3** Identifies circles, squares, triangles, ovals, diamonds, and rectangles in various orientations/positions.
LESSON 8.3 **2 DAYS** **Congruence** pp. 139A–140A **Objective** To identify and construct congruent figures	side corner	■ Problem Solving, ■ Reteach, ■ Practice, ■ Enrichment Worksheets 8.3 ▢ Transparencies Problem of the Day 8 Spiral Review 23	**QCC 1.9** Identifies relationships. **QCC 1.29** Selects elements belonging to or not belonging to a given set.
LESSON 8.4 **1 DAY** **Symmetry** pp. 141A–142A **Objective** To make symmetrical figures; to identify lines of symmetry	match	■ Problem Solving, ■ Reteach, ■ Practice, ■ Enrichment Worksheets 8.4 ▢ Transparencies Problem of the Day 8 Spiral Review 23	**QCC 1.6** Determines figures that are symmetrical by folding.

CHAPTER ASSESSMENT   Chapter 8 Review/Test p. 143–144

Chapter 9

Location and Movement

BIG IDEA
Geometric words and phrases can be used to describe location and movement.

PLANNING GUIDE

Introducing the Chapter p. 145   **School-Home Connection** p. 146

OBJECTIVE	VOCABULARY	RESOURCES	GEORGIA QCC OBJECTIVES
LESSON 9.1 **1 DAY** **Open and Closed** pp. 147A–148A Objective To identify open and closed figures	open closed	■ Problem Solving, ■ Reteach, ■ Practice, ■ Enrichment Worksheets 9.1 ▱ Transparencies Problem of the Day 9 Spiral Review 24	**QCC 1.29** Selects elements belonging to or not belonging to a given set. **QCC 1.38** Recalls addition facts and related subtraction facts presented vertically and horizontally.
LESSON 9.2 **1 DAY** **Inside, Outside, On** pp. 149A–150A Objective To identify and describe the terms *inside, outside,* and *on* in relation to closed plane figures	inside outside on	■ Problem Solving, ■ Reteach, ■ Practice, ■ Enrichment Worksheets 9.2 ◉ **Stanley's Sticker Stories,** p. 150A ▱ Transparencies Problem of the Day 9 Spiral Review 24	**QCC 1.5** Identifies a specified positional relationship between objects. **QCC 1.9** Identifies relationships.
LESSON 9.3 **2 DAYS** **Problem-Solving Strategy: Draw a Picture** pp. 151A–152A Objective To use directional terms *left* and *right* to describe location and solve problems	left right inside outside on	■ Reading Strategy • *Position Words,* ■ Reteach, ■ Practice, ■ Enrichment Worksheets 9.3 Problem-Solving Think Along, TR p. R113 ▱ Transparency Spiral Review 25	**QCC 1.5** Identifies a specified positional relationship between objects. **QCC 1.9** Identifies relationships.
LESSON 9.4 **1 DAY** **Positions on a Grid** pp. 153A–154A Objective To identify and describe positions at intersections of lines on a grid	right	■ Problem Solving, ■ Reteach, ■ Practice, ■ Enrichment Worksheets 9.4 ▱ Transparencies Problem of the Day 9 Spiral Review 25	**QCC 1.5** Identifies a specified positional relationship between objects. **QCC 1.9** Identifies relationships.

CHAPTER ASSESSMENT Chapter 9 Review/Test p. 155–156

Chapter 10 Patterns

BIG IDEA
Patterns can be described, reproduced, extended, and created.

PLANNING GUIDE

Introducing the Chapter p. 157 **School-Home Connection** p. 158

OBJECTIVE	VOCABULARY	RESOURCES	GEORGIA QCC OBJECTIVES
LESSON 10.1 **1 DAY** **Identifying Patterns** pp. 159A–160A Objective To identify, read, and extend patterns	pattern	▪ Problem Solving, ▪ Reteach, ▪ Practice, ▪ Enrichment Worksheets 10.1 ▫ Transparencies Problem of the Day 10 Spiral Review 26	**QCC 1.31** Continues simple patterns such as those involving numbers, shapes, colors, seasons, and events.
LESSON 10.2 **1 DAY** **Reproducing and Extending Patterns** pp. 161A–162A Objective To copy and extend patterns (AB, ABB, ABC)	pattern	▪ Problem Solving, ▪ Reteach, ▪ Practice, ▪ Enrichment Worksheets 10.2 ◉ **Stanley's Sticker Stories,** p. 162A ▫ Transparencies Problem of the Day 10 Spiral Review 26	**QCC 1.31** Continues simple patterns such as those involving numbers, shapes, colors, seasons, and events.
LESSON 10.3 **2 DAYS** **Making and Extending Patterns** pp. 163A–164A Objective To make and extend patterns	pattern	▪ Problem Solving, ▪ Reteach, ▪ Practice, ▪ Enrichment Worksheets 10.3 ◉ **Stanley's Sticker Stories,** p. 164A ▫ Transparencies Problem of the Day 10 Spiral Review 27	**QCC 1.31** Continues simple patterns such as those involving numbers, shapes, colors, seasons, and events.
LESSON 10.4 **1 DAY** **Problem Solving Strategy: Look for a Pattern** pp. 165A–166A Objective To use the problem-solving strategy *look for a pattern* to solve problems	pattern	▪ Reading Strategy • *Make Predictions,* ▪ Reteach, ▪ Practice, ▪ Enrichment Worksheets 10.4 Problem-Solving Think Along, TR p. R113 ▫ Transparencies Problem of the Day 10 Spiral Review 27	**QCC 1.31** Continues simple patterns such as those involving numbers, shapes, colors, seasons, and events. **QCC 1.36** Solves one- and two-step word problems.

CHAPTER ASSESSMENT Chapter 10 Review/Test p. 167–168

CHECKPOINT
Chapters 7–10 Math Fun p. 169, Technology, p. 170
Chapters 7–10 Take-Home Book pp. 170A–170B, Review/Test, pp. 171–172
Chapters 7–10 Performance Assessment p. 173
Chapters 1–10 Cumulative Review p. 174

Chapter 11 Addition Facts to 12

BIG IDEA
Addition names the whole when the parts are known.

PLANNING GUIDE

Introducing the Chapter p. 175 **School-Home Connection** p. 176

OBJECTIVE	VOCABULARY	RESOURCES	GEORGIA QCC OBJECTIVES
LESSON 11.1 **1 DAY** **Counting On to 12** pp. 177A–178A **Objective** To count on 1, 2, and 3 to find sums to 12	greater count on	■ Problem Solving, ■ Reteach, ■ Practice, ■ Enrichment Worksheets 11.1 ▢ Transparencies Problem of the Day 11 Spiral Review 28	**QCC 1.38** Recalls addition facts and related subtraction facts presented vertically and horizontally. **QCC 1.45** Determines addition and subtraction facts up to 18 using various strategies.
LESSON 11.2 **1 DAY** **Doubles to 12** pp. 179A–180A **Objective** To find the sums of doubles to 12	doubles sum	■ Problem Solving, ■ Reteach, ■ Practice, ■ Enrichment Worksheets 11.2 ◉ **Zoo Zillions •** *Number Line Express,* p. 180A ▢ Transparencies Problem of the Day 11 Spiral Review 28	**QCC 1.38** Recalls addition facts and related subtraction facts presented vertically and horizontally. **QCC 1.45** Determines addition and subtraction facts up to 18 using various strategies.
LESSON 11.3 **1 DAY** **Three Addends** pp. 181A–182A **Objective** To find the sum of three numbers; to explore the Associative Property	sum	■ Problem Solving, ■ Reteach, ■ Practice, ■ Enrichment Worksheets 11.3 ◉ **Carnival Countdown •** *Snap Clowns,* p. 182A ▢ Transparencies Problem of the Day 11 Spiral Review 29	**QCC 1.37** Adds three 1-digit whole numbers presented vertically and horizontally without regrouping.
LESSON 11.4 **1 DAY** **Practice the Facts** pp. 183A–184A **Objective** To practice basic addition facts to 12		■ Problem Solving, ■ Reteach, ■ Practice, ■ Enrichment Worksheets 11.4 ◉ **Zoo Zillions •** *Fish Stories,* p. 184A ▢ Transparencies Problem of the Day 11 Spiral Review 29	**QCC 1.37** Adds three 1-digit whole numbers presented vertically and horizontally without regrouping. **QCC 1.38** Recalls addition facts and related subtraction facts presented vertically and horizontally. **QCC 1.43** Explores the property of zero in addition and subtraction.
LESSON 11.5 **1 DAY** **Problem-Solving Strategy: Write a Number Sentence** pp. 185A–186A **Objective** To use the strategy *write a number sentence* to solve addition story problems	number sentence	■ Reading Strategy • Use Word Clues, ■ Reteach, ■ Practice, ■ Enrichment Worksheets 11.5 Problem-Solving Think Along, TR p. R113 ▢ Transparency Spiral Review 30	**QCC 1.36** Solves one- and two-step word problems. **QCC 1.41** Uses appropriate mathematical symbols (+, −, =).

CHAPTER ASSESSMENT   Chapter 11 Review/Test p. 187–188

Chapter 12 · Subtraction Facts to 12

BIG IDEA

Subtraction describes the process of subtracting from a whole.

PLANNING GUIDE

Introducing the Chapter p. 189 **School-Home Connection** p. 190

OBJECTIVE	VOCABULARY	RESOURCES	GEORGIA QCC OBJECTIVES
LESSON 12.1 **1 DAY** **Relating Addition and Subtraction** pp. 191A–192A Objective To find sums and related differences	addition sentence subtraction sentence	■ Problem Solving, ■ Reteach, ■ Practice, ■ Enrichment Worksheets 12.1 ▢ Transparencies Problem of the Day 12 Spiral Review 31	**QCC 1.38** Recalls addition facts and related subtraction facts presented vertically and horizontally.
LESSON 12.2 **1 DAY** **Counting Back** pp. 193A–194A Objective To count back 1, 2, and 3 to find differences	count back number line	■ Problem Solving, ■ Reteach, ■ Practice, ■ Enrichment Worksheets 12.2 ⊙ **Zoo Zillions** • *Number Line Express,* p. 194A ▢ Transparencies Problem of the Day 12 Spiral Review 31	**QCC 1.38** Recalls addition facts and related subtraction facts presented vertically and horizontally. **QCC 1.45** Determines addition and subtraction facts up to 18 using various strategies.
LESSON 12.3 **1 DAY** **Compare to Subtract** pp. 195A–196A Objective To solve comparative subtraction problems	compare more fewer	■ Problem Solving, ■ Reteach, ■ Practice, ■ Enrichment Worksheets 12.3 ⊙ **Zoo Zillions** • *Fish Stories,* p. 196A ▢ Transparencies Problem of the Day 12 Spiral Review 32	**QCC 1.38** Recalls addition facts and related subtraction facts presented vertically and horizontally.
LESSON 12.4 **1 DAY** **Fact Families** pp. 197A–198A Objective To identify and complete fact families	fact family	■ Problem Solving, ■ Reteach, ■ Practice, ■ Enrichment Worksheets 12.4 ▢ Transparencies Problem of the Day 12 Spiral Review 32	**QCC 1.38** Recalls addition facts and related subtraction facts presented vertically and horizontally.
LESSON 12.5 **1 DAY** **Problem-Solving Strategy: Write a Number Sentence** pp. 199A–200A Objective To use the strategy *write a number sentence* to solve addition and subtraction story problems	number sentence	■ Reading Strategy • *Reread,* ■ Reteach, ■ Practice, ■ Enrichment Worksheets 12.5 Problem-Solving Think Along, TR p. R113 ⊙ **Stanley's Sticker Stories,** p. 200A ▢ Transparency Spiral Review 33	**QCC 1.36** Solves one- and two-step word problems. **QCC 1.40** Adds and subtracts 2-digit whole numbers without regrouping vertically and horizontally.

CHAPTER ASSESSMENT Chapter 12 Review/Test p. 201–202

CHECKPOINT
Chapters 11–12 Math Fun, p. 203, Technology, p. 204
Chapters 11–12 Take-Home Book, pp. 204A–204B, Review/Test, pp. 205–206
Chapters 11–12 Performance Assessment, p. 207
Chapters 1–12 Cumulative Review, p. 208

Chapter 13 Building Numbers to 100

BIG IDEAS

Each whole number represents the cardinal number of a group. Numbers can be represented in different ways.

PLANNING GUIDE

Introducing the Chapter p. 209   **School-Home Connection** p. 210

OBJECTIVE	VOCABULARY	RESOURCES	GEORGIA QCC OBJECTIVES
LESSON 13.1 **1 DAY** **Tens** pp. 211A–212A **Objective** To model groups of 10; to count by tens; to write the numbers	tens	■ Problem Solving, ■ Reteach, ■ Practice, ■ Enrichment Worksheets 13.1 ▱ Transparencies Problem of the Day 13 Spiral Review 34	**QCC 1.21** Counts by ones, fives, and tens to 100 and by twos to 20. Counts backwards from 20.
LESSON 13.2 **1 DAY** **Tens and Ones to 20** pp. 213A–214A **Objective** To identify groups from 10 to 20; to write the numbers as tens and ones and as standard numerals	tens ones	■ Problem Solving, ■ Reteach, ■ Practice, ■ Enrichment Worksheets 13.2 ▱ Transparencies Problem of the Day 13 Spiral Review 34	**QCC 1.20** Selects the numeral that names a group of objects, and matches a group of objects with the appropriate numeral for a given set. **QCC 1.22** Models and pictorially represents whole numbers through 100 using groups of tens and ones and orally names numbers. **QCC 1.23** Translates words to numerals and numerals to words (0 through 20). **QCC 1.24** Recognizes, writes, and orally names numerals 0 through 100. **QCC 1.27** Identifies place value by determining number of tens and ones in a given number.
LESSON 13.3 **1 DAY** **Tens and Ones to 50** pp. 215A–216A **Objective** To write numbers from 20 to 50 as tens and ones and as standard numerals	tens ones	■ Problem Solving, ■ Reteach, ■ Practice, ■ Enrichment Worksheets 13.3 ◉ **Carnival Countdown •** *Bubble Band,* p. 216A ▱ Transparencies Problem of the Day 13 Spiral Review 35	**QCC 1.20** Selects the numeral that names a group of objects, and matches a group of objects with the appropriate numeral for a given set. **QCC 1.22** Models and pictorially represents whole numbers through 100 using groups of tens and ones and orally names numbers. **QCC 1.23** Translates words to numerals and numerals to words (0 through 20). **QCC 1.24** Recognizes, writes, and orally names numerals 0 through 100. **QCC 1.27** Identifies place value by determining number of tens and ones in a given number.
LESSON 13.4 **1 DAY** **Tens and Ones to 80** pp. 217A–218A **Objective** To count groups of objects; to write numbers to 80 as tens and ones and as standard numerals	tens ones	■ Problem Solving, ■ Reteach, ■ Practice, ■ Enrichment Worksheets 13.4 ◉ **Carnival Countdown •** *Bubble Band,* p. 218A ▱ Transparencies Problem of the Day 13 Spiral Review 35	**QCC 1.22** Models and pictorially represents whole numbers through 100 using groups of tens and ones and orally names numbers. **QCC 1.23** Translates words to numerals and numerals to words (0 through 20). **QCC 1.24** Recognizes, writes, and orally names numerals 0 through 100. **QCC 1.27** Identifies place value by determining number of tens and ones in a given number.
LESSON 13.5 **1 DAY** **Tens and Ones to 100** pp. 219A–220A **Objective** To model and identify groups of tens and ones to 100	tens ones	■ Problem Solving, ■ Reteach, ■ Practice, ■ Enrichment Worksheets 13.5 ◉ **Carnival Countdown •** *Bubble Band,* p. 220A ▱ Transparencies Problem of the Day 13 Spiral Review 36	**QCC 1.22** Models and pictorially represents whole numbers through 100 using groups of tens and ones and orally names numbers. **QCC 1.23** Translates word to numerals and numerals to words (0 through 20). **QCC 1.24** Recognizes, writes, and orally names numerals 0 through 100. **QCC 1.27** Identifies place value by determining number of tens and ones in a given number.
LESSON 13.6 **1 DAY** **Problem Solving: Use Estimation** pp. 221A–222A **Objective** To identify the better estimate when using 10 as a referent	estimate	■ Reading Strategy • *Using Sight Words,* ■ Reteach, ■ Practice, ■ Enrichment Worksheets 13.6 Problem-Solving Think Along, TR p. R113 ▱ Transparencies Problem of the Day 13 Spiral Review 36	**QCC 1.1** Explores estimation of quantities of less than 100.

CHAPTER ASSESSMENT Chapter 13 Review/Test p. 223–224

Chapter 14 Comparing and Ordering Numbers

BIG IDEA
Numbers can be compared and ordered.

PLANNING GUIDE

Introducing the Chapter p. 225   **School-Home Connection** p. 226

OBJECTIVE	VOCABULARY	RESOURCES	GEORGIA QCC OBJECTIVES
LESSON 14.1 **1 DAY** **Ordinals** pp. 227A–228A Objective To use ordinal number words to *twelfth*	order	■ Problem Solving, ■ Reteach, ■ Practice, ■ Enrichment Worksheets 14.1 ▢ Transparencies Problem of the Day 14 Spiral Review 37	**QCC 1.26** Uses ordinal numbers first through tenth to indicate position.
LESSON 14.2 **1 DAY** **Greater Than** pp. 229A–230A Objective To model and compare 2-digit numbers to determine which is greater	greater than	■ Problem Solving, ■ Reteach, ■ Practice, ■ Enrichment Worksheets 14.2 ◉ **Stanley's Sticker Stories,** p. 230A ▢ Transparencies Problem of the Day 14 Spiral Review 37	**QCC 1.22** Models and pictorially represents whole numbers through 100 using groups of tens and ones and orally names numbers. **QCC 1.28** Identifies numerical relations of numbers 0 through 100 and sequences of numbers in ascending order.
LESSON 14.3 **1 DAY** **Less Than** pp. 231A–232A Objective To model and compare 2-digit numbers to determine which is less	less than	■ Problem Solving, ■ Reteach, ■ Practice, ■ Enrichment Worksheets 14.3 ▢ Transparencies Problem of the Day 14 Spiral Review 38	**QCC 1.22** Models and pictorially represents whole numbers through 100 using groups of tens and ones and orally names numbers. **QCC 1.28** Identifies numerical relations of numbers 0 through 100 and sequences of numbers in ascending order.
LESSON 14.4 **1 DAY** **Before, After, Between** pp. 233A–234A Objective To model a series of 2-digit numbers to determine the missing number that comes before, after, or between	before, after, between	■ Problem Solving, ■ Reteach, ■ Practice, ■ Enrichment Worksheets 14.4 ▢ Transparencies Problem of the Day 14 Spiral Review 38	**QCC 1.32** Sequences numbers and points on a number line and determines missing numerals (0 through 20).
LESSON 14.5 **1 DAY** **Order to 100** pp. 235A–236A Objective To order a series of numbers from least to greatest	least, greatest, order	■ Problem Solving, ■ Reteach, ■ Practice, ■ Enrichment Worksheets 14.5 ◉ **Carnival Countdown •** *Giggle Factory,* p. 236A ▢ Transparencies Problem of the Day 14 Spiral Review 39	**QCC 1.28** Identifies numerical relations of numbers 0 through 100 and sequences of numbers in ascending order.

CHAPTER ASSESSMENT Chapter 14 Review/Test p. 237–238

Chapter 15 Patterns on a Hundreds Chart

BIG IDEA
Patterns show special relationships.

PLANNING GUIDE

Introducing the Chapter p. 239   **School-Home Connection** p. 240

OBJECTIVE	VOCABULARY	RESOURCES	GEORGIA QCC OBJECTIVES
LESSON 15.1 **1 DAY** **Counting by Tens** pp. 241A–242A Objective To count by tens	ten	■ Problem Solving, ■ Reteach, ■ Practice, ■ Enrichment Worksheets 15.1 ▣ Transparencies Problem of the Day 15 Spiral Review 40	**QCC 1.21** Counts by ones, fives, and tens to 100 and by twos to 20. Counts backwards from 20. **QCC 1.24** Recognizes, writes, and orally names numerals 0 through 100. **QCC 1.31** Continues simple patterns such as those involving numbers, shapes, colors, seasons, and events. **QCC 1.36** Solves one- and two-step word problems.
LESSON 15.2 **1 DAY** **Counting by Fives** pp. 243A–244A Objective To count by fives		■ Problem Solving, ■ Reteach, ■ Practice, ■ Enrichment Worksheets 15.2 ▣ Transparencies Problem of the Day 15 Spiral Review 40	**QCC 1.21** Counts by ones, fives, and tens to 100 and by twos to 20. Counts backwards from 20. **QCC 1.24** Recognizes, writes, and orally names numerals 0 through 100. **QCC 1.28** Identifies numerical relations of numbers 0 through 100 and sequences of numbers in ascending order. **QCC 1.31** Continues simple patterns such as those involving numbers, shapes, colors, seasons, and events. **QCC 1.37** Adds three 1-digit whole numbers presented vertically and horizontally without regrouping.
LESSON 15.3 **1 DAY** **Counting by Twos** pp. 245A–246A Objective To count by twos		■ Problem Solving, ■ Reteach, ■ Practice, ■ Enrichment Worksheets 15.3 ◎ **Zoo Zillions** • *Annie's Jungle Trail*, p. 246A ▣ Transparencies Problem of the Day 15 Spiral Review 41	**QCC 1.21** Counts by ones, fives, and tens to 100 and by twos to 20. Counts backwards from 20. **QCC 1.24** Recognizes, writes, and orally names numerals 0 through 100. **QCC 1.31** Continues simple patterns such as those involving numbers, shapes, colors, seasons, and events. **QCC 1.36** Solves one- and two-step word problems. **QCC 1.38** Recalls addition facts and related subtraction facts presented vertically and horizontally.
LESSON 15.4 **2 DAYS** **Even and Odd Numbers** pp. 247A–248A Objective To model and identify odd and even numbers	odd even	■ Problem Solving, ■ Reteach, ■ Practice, ■ Enrichment Worksheets 15.4 ▣ Transparencies Problem of the Day 15 Spiral Review 41	**QCC 1.24** Recognizes, writes, and orally names numerals 0 through 100. **QCC 1.30** Recognizes equivalent and nonequivalent sets using one-to-one correspondence. **QCC 1.36** Solves one- and two-step word problems. **QCC 1.38** Recalls addition facts and related subtraction facts presented vertically and horizontally.

CHAPTER ASSESSMENT Chapter 15 Review/Test p. 249–250

CHECKPOINT
Chapters 13–15 Math Fun p. 251, Technology p. 252
Chapters 13–15 Take-Home Book pp. 252A–252B, Review/Test pp. 253–254
Chapters 13–15 Performance Assessment p. 255
Chapters 1–15 Cumulative Review p. 256

Chapter 16 Counting Pennies, Nickels, and Dimes

BIG IDEA
Numbers can be used to count, order, and name. Equal quantities can be represented in a variety of ways.

PLANNING GUIDE

Introducing the Chapter p. 257 **School-Home Connection** p. 258

OBJECTIVE	VOCABULARY	RESOURCES	GEORGIA QCC OBJECTIVES
LESSON 16.1 **1 DAY** **Pennies and Nickels** pp. 259A–260A **Objective** To identify the penny and nickel and their values; to count collections of pennies and nickels	penny nickel	■ Problem Solving, ■ Reteach, ■ Practice, ■ Enrichment Worksheets 16.1 ▨ Transparencies Problem of the Day 16 Spiral Review 42	**QCC 1.12** Names and identifies values of coins and dollar bills. **QCC 1.13** Determines the value of a set of coins up to $0.50. **QCC 1.14** Determines equivalent values of coins up to $0.50. **QCC 1.36** Solves one- and two-step word problems.
LESSON 16.2 **1 DAY** **Pennies and Dimes** pp. 261A–262A **Objective** To identify the dime and its value in pennies; to count collections of only dimes to 90¢	dime penny (pennies) tens amount cent (cents)	■ Problem Solving, ■ Reteach, ■ Practice, ■ Enrichment Worksheets 16.2 ▨ Transparencies Problem of the Day 16 Spiral Review 42	**QCC 1.12** Names and identifies values of coins and dollar bills. **QCC 1.13** Determines the value of a set of coins up to $0.50. **QCC 1.37** Adds three 1-digit whole numbers presented vertically and horizontally without regrouping. **QCC 1.38** Recalls addition facts and related subtraction facts presented vertically and horizontally.
LESSON 16.3 **1 DAY** **Counting Collections of Nickels and Pennies** pp. 263A–264A **Objective** To count mixed collections of pennies and nickels to 49¢	penny nickel dime ones amount	■ Problem Solving, ■ Reteach, ■ Practice, ■ Enrichment Worksheets 16.3 ◉ **Zoo Zillions •** *Gnu Ewe Boutique*, p. 264A ▨ Transparencies Problem of the Day 16 Spiral Review 43	**QCC 1.13** Determines the value of a set of coins up to $0.50. **QCC 1.14** Determines equivalent values of coins up to $0.50. **QCC 1.36** Solves one- and two-step word problems. **QCC 1.37** Adds three 1-digit whole numbers presented vertically and horizontally without regrouping.
LESSON 16.4 **1 DAY** **Counting Collections of Dimes and Pennies** pp. 265A–266A **Objective** To count mixed collections ofpennies and dimes to 65¢	penny nickel dime tens ones amount count on	■ Problem Solving, ■ Reteach, ■ Practice, ■ Enrichment Worksheets 16.4 ▨ Transparencies Problem of the Day 16 Spiral Review 43	**QCC 1.13** Determines the value of a set of coins up to $0.50. **QCC 1.21** Counts by ones, fives, and tens to 100 and by twos to 20. Counts backwards from 20. **QCC 1.22** Models and pictorially represents whole numbers through 100 using groups of tens and ones and orally names numbers. **QCC 1.28** Identifies numerical relations of numbers 0 through 100 and sequences of numbers in ascending order. **QCC 1.36** Solves one- and two-step word problems.
LESSON 16.5 **1 DAY** **Problem Solving: Choose the Model** pp. 267A–268A **Objective** To choose a model to solve problems		■ Reading Strategy • Using Pictures ■ Reteach, ■ Practice, ■ Enrichment Worksheets 16.5 Problem-Solving Think Along, TR p. R113 ▨ Spiral Review 44	**QCC 1.12** Names and identifies values of coins and dollar bills. **QCC 1.13** Determines the value of a set of coins up to $0.50. **QCC 1.14** Determines equivalent values of coins up to $0.50. **QCC 1.21** Counts by ones, fives, and tens to 100 and by twos to 20. Counts backwards from 20. **QCC 1.41** Uses appropriate mathematical symbols $(+, -, =)$.

CHAPTER ASSESSMENT *Chapter 16 Review/Test p. 269–270*

Chapter 17 Using Pennies, Nickels, and Dimes

BIG IDEA
Equal quantities can be shown in a variety of ways. Equal amounts can be exchanged.

PLANNING GUIDE

Introducing the Chapter p. 271   **School-Home Connection** p. 272

OBJECTIVE	VOCABULARY	RESOURCES	GEORGIA QCC OBJECTIVES
LESSON 17.1 **1 DAY** **Trading Pennies, Nickels, and Dimes** pp. 273A–274A Objective To trade coins to show the same money amount, using different coin combinations	trade fewest penny nickel dime	■ Problem Solving, ■ Reteach, ■ Practice, ■ Enrichment Worksheets 17.1 ◉ Zoo Zillions • *Gnu Ewe Boutique*, p. 274A ▱ Transparencies Problem of the Day 17 Spiral Review 45	**QCC 1.12** Names and identifies values of coins and dollar bills. **QCC 1.13** Determines the value of a set of coins up to $0.50. **QCC 1.14** Determines equivalent values of coins up to $0.50. **QCC 1.21** Counts by ones, fives, and tens to 100 and by twos to 20. Counts backwards from 20. **QCC 1.31** Continues simple patterns such as those involving numbers, shapes, colors, seasons, and events.
LESSON 17.2 **1 DAY** **Equal Amounts** pp. 275A–276A Objective To identify prices and show the same amount, using fewer coins	amount fewer	■ Problem Solving, ■ Reteach, ■ Practice, ■ Enrichment Worksheets 17.2 ▱ Transparencies Problem of the Day 17 Spiral Review 45	**QCC 1.12** Names and identifies values of coins and dollar bills. **QCC 1.13** Determines the value of a set of coins up to $0.50. **QCC 1.14** Determines equivalent values of coins up to $0.50. **QCC 1.21** Counts by ones, fives, and tens to 100 and by twos to 20. Counts backwards from 20. **QCC 1.32** Sequences numbers and points on a number line and determines missing numerals (0 through 20). **QCC 1.36** Solves one- and two-step word problems.
LESSON 17.3 **1 DAY** **How Much Is Needed?** pp. 277A–278A Objective To identify the fewest coins needed to purchase an item	coins fewest	■ Problem Solving, ■ Reteach, ■ Practice, Enrichment Worksheets 17.3 ▱ Transparencies Problem of the Day 17 Spiral Review 46	**QCC 1.13** Determines the value of a set of coins up to $0.50. **QCC 1.14** Determines equivalent values of coins up to $0.50. **QCC 1.21** Counts by ones, fives, and tens to 100 and by twos to 20. Counts backwards from 20. **QCC 1.36** Solves one- and two-step word problems.
LESSON 17.4 **1 DAY** **Quarter** pp. 279A–280A Objective To identify the quarter and its value and model different ways to make 25 cents	quarter coins amount equal	■ Problem Solving, ■ Reteach, ■ Practice, ■ Enrichment Worksheets 17.4 ▱ Transparencies Problem of the Day 17 Spiral Review 46	**QCC 1.12** Names and identifies values of coins and dollar bills. **QCC 1.13** Determines the value of a set of coins up to $0.50. **QCC 1.14** Determines equivalent values of coins up to $0.50.
LESSON 17.5 **1 DAY** **Problem-Solving Strategy: Act It Out** pp. 281A–282A Objective To use the strategy *act it out* to solve problems related to buying items	coins fewest	■ Reading Strategy • *Make Predictions*, ■ Reteach, ■ Practice, ■ Enrichment Worksheets 14.5 Problem-Solving Think Along, TR p. R113 ▱ Transparency Spiral Review 47	**QCC 1.13** Determines the value of a set of coins up to $0.50. **QCC 1.14** Determines equivalent values of coins up to $0.50. **QCC 1.36** Solves one- and two-step word problems. **QCC 1.38** Recalls addition facts and related subtraction facts presented vertically and horizontally.

CHAPTER ASSESSMENT   **Chapter 17 Review/Test p. 283–284**

BIG IDEA
Measurement can be used to impose order on objects and events.

PLANNING GUIDE

Introducing the Chapter p. 285   **School-Home Connection** p. 286

OBJECTIVE	VOCABULARY	RESOURCES	GEORGIA QCC OBJECTIVES
LESSON 18.1 **1 DAY** **Ordering Months and Days** pp. 287A–288A **Objective** To identify and order the 12 months	**trade** fewest penny nickel dime	■ Problem Solving, ■ Reteach, ■ Practice, ■ Enrichment Worksheets 18.1 ▱ Transparencies Problem of the Day 18 Spiral Review 48	**QCC 1.15** Identifies days, weeks, and months on a calendar. **QCC 1.16** Identifies number of minutes in an hour, number of days in a week, and number of months in a year. **QCC 1.17** Selects appropriate units and appropriate instruments (clocks and calendars) to measure time.
LESSON 18.2 **1 DAY** **Problem Solving: Using a Calendar** pp. 289A–290A **Objective** To use the problem-solving strategy *using a calendar* to solve problems	**calendar** **date** month days	■ Reading Strategy • *Matching Text,* ■ Reteach, ■ Practice, ■ Enrichment Worksheets 18.2 Problem-Solving Think Along, TR p. 113 ▱ Transparencies Problem of the Day 18 Spiral Review 48	**QCC 1.13** Determines the value of a set of coins up to $0.50. **QCC 1.15** Identifies days, weeks, and months on a calendar. **QCC 1.16** Identifies number of minutes in an hour, number of days in a week, and number of months in a year. **QCC 1.21** Counts by ones, fives, and tens to 100 and by twos to 20. Counts backwards from 20.
LESSON 18.3 **1 DAY** **Ordering Events** pp. 291A–292A **Objective** To sequence daily and weekly events		■ Problem Solving, ■ Reteach, ■ Practice, ■ Enrichment Worksheets 18.3 ◉ **Stanley's Sticker Stories,** p. 292A ▱ Transparencies Problem of the Day 18 Spiral Review 49	**QCC 1.16** Identifies number of minutes in an hour, number of days in a week, and number of months in a year. **QCC 1.17** Selects appropriate units and appropriate instruments (clocks and calendars) to measure time.
LESSON 18.4 **1 DAY** **Problem Solving: Estimating Time** pp. 293A–294A **Objective** To use the problem-solving strategy *estimating time* to solve problems		■ Reading Strategy • *Use Prior Knowledge,* ■ Reteach, ■ Practice, ■ Enrichment Worksheets 18.4 Problem-Solving Think Along, TR p. 113 ▱ Transparencies Problem of the Day 18 Spiral Review 49	**QCC 1.17** Selects appropriate units and appropriate instruments (clocks and calendars) to measure time.

CHAPTER ASSESSMENT   Chapter 18 Review/Test p. 295–296

Chapter 19 Telling Time

BIG IDEA

Measurement can be used to impose order on objects and events.

PLANNING GUIDE

Introducing the Chapter p. 297   **School-Home Connection** p. 298

OBJECTIVE	VOCABULARY	RESOURCES	GEORGIA QCC OBJECTIVES
LESSON 19.1 **1 DAY** **Reading the Clock** pp. 299A–300A Objective To identify the parts of a clock; to write the time to the hour	minute hand hour hand o'clock	■ Problem Solving, ■ Reteach, ■ Practice, ■ Enrichment Worksheets 19.1 ⬛ Transparencies Problem of the Day 19 Spiral Review 50	**QCC 1.18** Tells time to the half-hour and hour.
LESSON 19.2 **1 DAY** **Hour** pp. 301A–302A Objective To read the time on an analog clock; to write the time for a digital clock	hour	■ Problem Solving, ■ Reteach, ■ Practice, ■ Enrichment Worksheets 19.2 ⬤ **Stanley's Sticker Stories,** p. 302A ⬛ Transparencies Problem of the Day 19 Spiral Review 50	**QCC 1.18** Tells time to the half-hour and hour.
LESSON 19.3 **1 DAY** **Time to the Hour** pp. 303A–304A Objective To identify the time on a digital clock; to show time from a digital clock the way it looks on an analog clock	minute hand hour hand	■ Problem Solving, ■ Reteach, ■ Practice, ■ Enrichment Worksheets 19.3 ⬤ **Stanley's Sticker Stories,** p. 304A ⬛ Transparencies Problem of the Day 19 Spiral Review 51	**QCC 1.18** Tells time to the half-hour and hour.
LESSON 19.4 **1 DAY** **Half Hour** pp. 305A–306A Objective To read a clock that shows time to the half hour	half hour minutes after minute hand hour hand	■ Problem Solving, ■ Reteach, ■ Practice, ■ Enrichment Worksheets 19.4 ⬛ Transparencies Problem of the Day 19 Spiral Review 51	**QCC 1.18** Tells time to the half-hour and hour.
LESSON 19.5 **1 DAY** **Problem-Solving Strategy: Act It Out** pp. 307A–308A Objective To use the problem-solving strategy *act it out* to estimate the passage of 1 minute		■ Reading Strategy • *Using Context Clues,* ■ Reteach, ■ Practice, ■ Enrichment Worksheets 19.5 Problem-Solving Think Along, TR p. R113 ⬛ Transparency Spiral Review 52	**QCC 1.17** Selects appropriate units and appropriate instruments (clocks and calendars) to measure time. **QCC 1.31** Continues simple patterns such as those involving numbers, shapes, colors, seasons, and events.

CHAPTER ASSESSMENT Chapter 19 Review/Test p. 309–310

CHECKPOINT
- **Chapters 16–19 Math Fun p. 311, Technology, p. 312**
- **Chapters 16–19 Take-Home Book pp. 312A–312B, Review/Test, pp. 313–314**
- **Chapters 16–19 Performance Assessment p. 315**
- **Chapters 16–19 Cumulative Review, p. 316**

Chapter 20 Measuring Length

BIG IDEA

The number of units can be determined by counting equivalent nonstandard and standard units and by reading a measuring tool.

PLANNING GUIDE

Introducing the Chapter p. 317   **School-Home Connection** p. 318

OBJECTIVE	VOCABULARY	RESOURCES	GEORGIA QCC OBJECTIVES
LESSON 20.1 **1 DAY** **Using Nonstandard Units** pp. 319A–320A Objective To estimate and measure length; to use nonstandard units	measure long	■ Problem Solving, ■ Reteach, ■ Practice, ■ Enrichment Worksheets 20.1 ● Stanley's Sticker Stories, p. 320A ▢ Transparencies Problem of the Day 20 Spiral Review 53	**QCC 1.18** Tells time to the half-hour and hour.
LESSON 20.2 **1 DAY** **Measuring in Inch Units** pp. 321A–322A Objective To use concrete models for inch units; to estimate and measure using inch units	inch long	■ Problem Solving, ■ Reteach, ■ Practice, ■ Enrichment Worksheets 20.2 ▢ Transparencies Problem of the Day 20 Spiral Review 53	**QCC 1.10** Describes, orders, and measures length using inches and centimeters.
LESSON 20.3 **1 DAY** **Using an Inch Ruler** pp. 323A–324A Objective To estimate and measure length to the nearest inch; to use an inch ruler	inch measure long	■ Problem Solving, ■ Reteach, ■ Practice, ■ Enrichment Worksheets 20.3 ▢ Transparencies Problem of the Day 20 Spiral Review 54	**QCC 1.1** Explores estimation of quantities of less than 100. **QCC 1.10** Describes, orders, and measures length using inches and centimeters.
LESSON 20.4 **1 DAY** **Measuring in Centimeter Units** pp. 325A–326A Objective To use concrete models for centimeter units; to estimate and measure using centimeter units	centimeter long	■ Problem Solving, ■ Reteach, ■ Practice, ■ Enrichment Worksheets 20.4 ● Stanley's Sticker Stories, p. 326A ▢ Transparencies Problem of the Day 20 Spiral Review 54	**QCC 1.10** Describes, orders, and measures length using inches and centimeters.
LESSON 20.5 **1 DAY** **Using a Centimeter Ruler** pp. 327A–328A Objective To estimate and measure length to the nearest centimeter; to use a centimeter ruler	centimeter measure long estimate	■ Problem Solving, ■ Reteach, ■ Practice, ■ Enrichment Worksheets 20.5 ▢ Transparencies Problem of the Day 20 Spiral Review 55	**QCC 1.10** Describes, orders, and measures length using inches and centimeters.

CHAPTER ASSESSMENT   Chapter 20 Review/Test p. 329–330

Chapter 21 — Measuring Mass, Capacity, and Temperature

BIG IDEA
The process of measuring is identical for any attribute: choose the unit, compare the unit to what is being measured, and report the number of units.

PLANNING GUIDE

Introducing the Chapter p. 331   **School-Home Connection** p. 332

OBJECTIVE	VOCABULARY	RESOURCES	GEORGIA QCC OBJECTIVES
LESSON 21.1 **1 DAY** **Using a Balance** pp. 333A–334A Objective To estimate and compare weights	heavier lighter estimate measure	■ Problem Solving, ■ Reteach, ■ Practice, ■ Enrichment Worksheets 21.1 ● **Stanley's Sticker Stories,** p. 334A ▢ Transparencies Problem of the Day 21 Spiral Review 56	**QCC 1.1** Explores estimation of quantities of less than 100. **QCC 1.19** Compares weight of two real objects and capacity of two real containers, and compares the height of two real objects.
LESSON 21.2 **1 DAY** **Problem-Solving Strategy: Guess and Check** pp. 335A–336A Objective To use the strategy *guess and check* to solve problems	scale balance estimate measure	■ Reading Strategy • *Make Predictions,* ■ Reteach, ■ Practice, ■ Enrichment Worksheets 21.2 Problem-Solving Think Along, TR p. R113 ▢ Transparencies Problem of the Day 21 Spiral Review 56	**QCC 1.1** Explores estimation of quantities of less than 100. **QCC 1.19** Compares weight of two real objects and capacity of two real containers, and compares the height of two real objects.
LESSON 21.3 **2 DAYS** **Measuring with Cups** pp. 337A–338A Objective To estimate and measure capacity	estimate measure	■ Problem Solving, ■ Reteach, ■ Practice, ■ Enrichment Worksheets 21.3 ▢ Transparencies Problem of the Day 21 Spiral Review 57	**QCC 1.1** Explores estimation of quantities of less than 100. **QCC 1.19** Compares weight of two real objects and capacity of two real containers, and compares the height of two real objects.
LESSON 21.4 **1 DAY** **Temperature: Hot and Cold** pp. 339A–340A Objective To estimate and compare temperatures	hot cold	■ Problem Solving, ■ Reteach, ■ Practice, ■ Enrichment Worksheets 21.4 ▢ Transparencies Problem of the Day 21 Spiral Review 57	**QCC 1.9** Identifies relationships.

CHAPTER ASSESSMENT Chapter 21 Review/Test p. 341–342

Chapter 22 Fractions

BIG IDEA
A fraction is a relationship between a part and a whole.

PLANNING GUIDE

Introducing the Chapter p. 343 **School-Home Connection** p. 344

OBJECTIVE	VOCABULARY	RESOURCES	GEORGIA QCC OBJECTIVES
LESSON 22.1 **1 DAY** **Equal and Unequal Parts of Wholes** pp. 345A–346A **Objective** To identify equal and unequal parts of wholes	equal parts	■ Problem Solving, ■ Reteach, ■ Practice, ■ Enrichment Worksheets 22.1 ⊙ **Carnival Countdown •** *Pattern Block Roundup*, p. 346A ▢ Transparencies Problem of the Day 22 Spiral Review 58	**QCC 1.2** Recognizes different ways of representing fractions using concrete and pictorial models and words for one-half and one-forth. **QCC 1.9** Identifies relationships.
LESSON 22.2 **1 DAY** **Halves** pp. 347A–348A **Objective** To identify halves and $\frac{1}{2}$ of wholes	halves one half $\frac{1}{2}$ whole	■ Problem Solving, ■ Reteach, ■ Practice, ■ Enrichment Worksheets 22.2 ▢ Transparencies Problem of the Day 22 Spiral Review 58	**QCC 1.2** Recognizes different ways of representing fractions using concrete and pictorial models and words for one-half and one-forth.
LESSON 22.3 **1 DAY** **Fourths** pp. 349A–350A **Objective** To identify fourths and $\frac{1}{4}$ of wholes	one third $\frac{1}{3}$ thirds whole parts fraction	■ Problem Solving, ■ Reteach, ■ Practice, ■ Enrichment Worksheets 22.3 ⊙ **Carnival Countdown •** *Pattern Block Roundup*, p. 350A ▢ Transparencies Problem of the Day 22 Spiral Review 59	**QCC 1.2** Recognizes different ways of representing fractions using concrete and pictorial models and words for one-half and one-forth.
LESSON 22.4 **1 DAY** **Thirds** pp. 351A–352A **Objective** To identify thirds and $\frac{1}{3}$ of wholes	hot cold	■ Problem Solving, ■ Reteach, ■ Practice, ■ Enrichment Worksheets 22.4 ▢ Transparencies Problem of the Day 22 Spiral Review 59	**QCC 1.2** Recognizes different ways of representing fractions using concrete and pictorial models and words for one-half and one-forth.
LESSON 22.5 **1 DAY** **Problem-Solving: Visualizing Results** pp. 353A–354A **Objective** To solve problems by visualizing results	share	■ Reading Strategy • *Visualize*, ■ Reteach, ■ Practice, ■ Enrichment Worksheets 22.5 Problem Solving Think Along, TR R113 ⊙ **Carnival Countdown •** *Pattern Block Roundup*, p. 354A ▢ Transparencies Problem of the Day 22 Spiral Review 60	**QCC 1.2** Recognizes different ways of representing fractions using concrete and pictorial models and words for one-half and one-forth. **QCC 1.6** Determines figures that are symmetrical by folding.
LESSON 22.6 **1 DAY** **Parts of Groups** pp. 355A–356A **Objective** To identify $\frac{1}{2}$, $\frac{1}{3}$, and $\frac{1}{4}$ of a group	equal parts fraction	■ Problem Solving, ■ Reteach, ■ Practice, ■ Enrichment Worksheets 22.6 ▢ Transparencies Problem of the Day 22 Spiral Review 60	**QCC 1.2** Recognizes different ways of representing fractions using concrete and pictorial models and words for one-half and one-forth.

CHAPTER ASSESSMENT Chapter 22 Review/Test p. 357–358

CHECKPOINT
Chapters 20–22 Math Fun p. 359, Technology p. 360
Chapters 20–22 Take-Home Book pp. 360A–360B, Review/Test pp. 361–362
Chapters 20–22 Performance Assessment p. 363
Chapters 1–22 Cumulative Review p. 364

Chapter 23 Organizing Data

PLANNING GUIDE

Introducing the Chapter p. 365   **School-Home Connection** p. 366

OBJECTIVE	VOCABULARY	RESOURCES	GEORGIA QCC OBJECTIVES
LESSON 23.1 **1 DAY** **Sort and Classify** pp. 367A–368A Objective To sort objects into two categories and make a tally table	sort tally mark table	■ Problem Solving, ■ Reteach, ■ Practice, ■ Enrichment Worksheets 23.1 Graph Links Plus, p. 368A Transparencies Problem of the Day 23 Spiral Review 61	**QCC 1.33** Organizes elements of sets according to characteristics such as use, size, and shape. **QCC 1.34** Interprets data by reading bar graphs and pictographs using whole unit data.
LESSON 23.2 **1 DAY** **Certain or Impossible** pp. 369A–370A Objective To predict if an event is certain or impossible	certain impossible	■ Problem Solving, ■ Reteach, ■ Practice, ■ Enrichment Worksheets 23.2 Transparencies Problem of the Day 23 Spiral Review 61	**QCC 1.29** Selects elements belonging to or not belonging to a given set.
LESSON 23.3 **1 DAY** **Most Likely** pp. 371A–372A Objective To collect and use data to predict which event is most likely to happen	most often tally	■ Problem Solving, ■ Reteach, ■ Practice, ■ Enrichment Worksheets 23.3 Graph Links Plus, p. 372A Transparencies Problem of the Day 23 Spiral Review 62	**QCC 1.28** Identifies numerical relations of numbers 0 through 100 and sequences of numbers in ascending order. **QCC 1.34** Interprets data by reading bar graphs and pictographs using whole unit data.
LESSON 23.4 **2 DAYS** **Problem-Solving Strategy: Use a Table** pp. 373A–374A Objective To use the problem-solving strategy *use a table*	predict tally	■ Reading Strategy • Use Graphic Aids, ■ Reteach, ■ Practice, ■ Enrichment Worksheets 23.4 Problem-Solving Think Along, TR p. R113 Transparencies Problem of the Day 23 Spiral Review 62	**QCC 1.34** Interprets data by reading bar graphs and pictographs using whole unit data. **QCC 1.36** Solves one- and two-step word problems.

CHAPTER ASSESSMENT   Chapter 23 Review/Test p. 375–376

BIG IDEA

Information can be collected and displayed as objects, pictures, graphs, and tables.

PLANNING GUIDE

Introducing the Chapter p. 377 **School-Home Connection** p. 378

OBJECTIVE	VOCABULARY	RESOURCES	GEORGIA QCC OBJECTIVES
LESSON 24.1 **1 DAY** **Picture Graphs** pp. 379A–380A Objective To make and interpret picture graphs	picture graph	■ Problem Solving, ■ Reteach, ■ Practice, ■ Enrichment Worksheets 24.1 Harcourt Brace Computer Links, Graph Links, p. 380A Transparencies Problem of the Day 24 Spiral Review 63	**QCC 1.29** Selects elements belonging to or not belonging to a given set. **QCC 1.34** Interprets data by reading bar graphs and pictographs using whole unit data. **QCC 1.35** Constructs simple graphs using concrete objects such as blocks and squares.
LESSON 24.2 **1 DAY** **Problem Solving: Use Data from a Graph** pp. 381A–382A Objective To use the problem-solving strategy *use data from a graph* to make and interpret horizontal bar graphs	bar graph tally	■ Reading Strategy • *Compare and Contrast,* ■ Reteach, ■ Practice, ■ Enrichment Worksheets 24.2 Problem-Solving Think Along, TR p. R113 Transparencies Problem of the Day 24 Spiral Review 63	**QCC 1.34** Interprets data by reading bar graphs and pictographs using whole unit data. **QCC 1.35** Constructs simple graphs using concrete objects such as blocks and squares.
LESSON 24.3 **1 DAY** **Vertical Bar Graphs** pp. 383A–384A Objective To make and interpret vertical bar graphs	bar graph tally	■ Problem Solving, ■ Reteach, ■ Practice, ■ Enrichment Worksheets 24.3 Transparencies Problem of the Day 24 Spiral Review 64	**QCC 1.34** Interprets data by reading bar graphs and pictographs using whole unit data. **QCC 1.35** Constructs simple graphs using concrete objects such as blocks and squares.
LESSON 24.4 **2 DAYS** **Problem-Solving Strategy: Make a Graph** pp. 385A–386A Objective To use the problem-solving strategy *make a graph* to display collected data and to answer a question	tally bar graph	■ Reading Strategy • *Use Graphic Aids,* ■ Reteach, ■ Practice, ■ Enrichment Worksheets 24.4 Problem-Solving Think Along, TR p. R113 Harcourt Brace Computer Links, Graph Links, p. 386A Transparency Spiral Review 64	**QCC 1.34** Interprets data by reading bar graphs and pictographs using whole unit data. **QCC 1.35** Constructs simple graphs using concrete objects such as blocks and squares.

CHAPTER ASSESSMENT Chapter 24 Review/Test p. 387–388

CHECKPOINT
Chapters 23–24 Math Fun p. 389, Technology p. 390
Chapters 23–24 Take-Home Book pp. 390A–390B, Review/Test pp. 391–392
Chapters 23–24 Performance Assessment p. 393
Chapters 1–24 Cumulative Review p. 394

Chapter 25 Facts to 18

BIG IDEA
Thinking strategies can relate known facts to unknown facts.

PLANNING GUIDE

Introducing the Chapter p. 395 | **School-Home Connection** p. 396

OBJECTIVE	VOCABULARY	RESOURCES	GEORGIA QCC OBJECTIVES
LESSON 25.1 **1 DAY** **Doubles Plus One** pp. 397A–398A **Objective** To use doubles facts to identify sums of doubles-plus-one facts	doubles plus one sum doubles	■ Problem Solving, ■ Reteach, ■ Practice, ■ Enrichment Worksheets 25.1 ▭ Transparencies Problem of the Day 25 Spiral Review 65	**QCC 1.36** Solves one- and two-step word problems. **QCC 1.38** Recalls addition facts and related subtraction facts presented vertically and horizontally. **QCC 1.45** Determines addition and subtraction facts up to 18 using various strategies.
LESSON 25.2 **1 DAY** **Doubles Minus One** pp. 399A–400A **Objective** To use doubles to identify doubles-minus-one facts to 18	doubles minus one sum doubles	■ Problem Solving, ■ Reteach, ■ Practice, ■ Enrichment Worksheets 25.2 ▭ Transparencies Problem of the Day 25 Spiral Review 65	**QCC 1.36** Solves one- and two-step word problems. **QCC 1.38** Recalls addition facts and related subtraction facts presented vertically and horizontally. **QCC 1.45** Determines addition and subtraction facts up to 18 using various strategies.
LESSON 25.3 **1 DAY** **Doubles Patterns** pp. 401A–402A **Objective** To identify doubles, doubles-plus-one, and doubles-minus-one fact patterns	doubles doubles plus one doubles minus one pattern	■ Problem Solving, ■ Reteach, ■ Practice, ■ Enrichment Worksheets 25.3 ◉ **Carnival Countdown** • *Snap Clowns,* p. 402A ▭ Transparencies Problem of the Day 25 Spiral Review 66	**QCC 1.36** Solves one- and two-step word problems. **QCC 1.38** Recalls addition facts and related subtraction facts presented vertically and horizontally. **QCC 1.44** Relates addition and subtraction to words, pictures, and concrete models. **QCC 1.45** Determines addition and subtraction facts up to 18 using various strategies.
LESSON 25.4 **1 DAY** **Doubles Fact Families** pp. 403A–404A **Objective** To identify doubles fact families using doubles	fact family doubles sum difference	■ Problem Solving, ■ Reteach, ■ Practice, ■ Enrichment Worksheets 25.4 ▭ Transparencies Problem of the Day 25 Spiral Review 66	**QCC 1.36** Solves one- and two-step word problems. **QCC 1.38** Recalls addition facts and related subtraction facts presented vertically and horizontally. **QCC 1.44** Relates addition and subtraction to words, pictures, and concrete models. **QCC 1.45** Determines addition and subtraction facts up to 18 using various strategies.
LESSON 25.5 **1 DAY** **Problem-Solving Strategy: Make a Model** pp. 405A–406A **Objective** To use the strategy *make a model* to solve problems		■ Reading Strategy • *Use Word Clues,* ■ Reteach, ■ Practice, ■ Enrichment Worksheets 25.5 Problem-Solving Think Along, TR p. R113 ◉ **Zoo Zillions** • *Fish Stories,* p. 406A ▭ Transparency Spiral Review 67	**QCC 1.36** Solves one- and two-step word problems. **QCC 1.38** Recalls addition facts and related subtraction facts presented vertically and horizontally. **QCC 1.44** Relates addition and subtraction to words, pictures, and concrete models.

CHAPTER ASSESSMENT   Chapter 25 Review/Test p. 407–408

More About Facts to 18

BIG IDEA
Thinking strategies can relate known facts to unknown facts.

PLANNING GUIDE

Introducing the Chapter p. 409   **School-Home Connection** p. 410

OBJECTIVE	VOCABULARY	RESOURCES	GEORGIA QCC OBJECTIVES
LESSON 26.1 **2 DAYS** **Make a Ten** pp. 411A–412A Objective To solve addition facts to 18, using the *make-a-ten* strategy	greater	■ Problem Solving, ■ Reteach, ■ Practice, ■ Enrichment Worksheets 26.1 ⬜ Transparencies Problem of the Day 26 Spiral Review 68	**QCC 1.36** Solves one- and two-step word problems. **QCC 1.38** Recalls addition facts and related subtraction facts presented vertically and horizontally. **QCC 1.44** Relates addition and subtraction to words, pictures, and concrete models. **QCC 1.45** Determines addition and subtraction facts up to 18 using various strategies.
LESSON 26.2 **1 DAY** **Adding Three Numbers** pp. 413A–414A Objective To find the sum of three addends by using doubles and names for 10	doubles	■ Problem Solving, ■ Reteach, ■ Practice, ■ Enrichment Worksheets 26.2 💿 **Carnival Countdown •** *Snap Clowns,* p. 414A ⬜ Transparencies Problem of the Day 26 Spiral Review 68	**QCC 1.37** Adds three 1-digit whole numbers presented vertically and horizontally without regrouping.
LESSON 26.3 **1 DAY** **Sums and Differences to 14** pp. 415A–416A Objective To find sums and differences to 14		■ Problem Solving, ■ Reteach, ■ Practice, ■ Enrichment Worksheets 26.3 💿 **Zoo Zillions •** *Fish Stories,* p. 416A ⬜ Transparencies Problem of the Day 26 Spiral Review 69	**QCC 1.25** Recognizes different names for whole numbers through 20. **QCC 1.36** Solves one- and two-step word problems. **QCC 1.37** Adds three 1-digit whole numbers presented vertically and horizontally without regrouping. **QCC 1.38** Recalls addition facts and related subtraction facts presented vertically and horizontally. **QCC 1.44** Relates addition and subtraction to words, pictures, and concrete models.
LESSON 26.4 **1 DAY** **Sums and Differences to 18** pp. 417A–418A Objective To find sums and differences to 18	sum difference	■ Problem Solving, ■ Reteach, ■ Practice, ■ Enrichment Worksheets 26.4 ⬜ Transparencies Problem of the Day 26 Spiral Review 69	**QCC 1.25** Recognizes different names for whole numbers through 20. **QCC 1.36** Solves one- and two-step word problems. **QCC 1.38** Recalls addition facts and related subtraction facts presented vertically and horizontally. **QCC 1.44** Relates addition and subtraction to words, pictures, and concrete models.

CHAPTER ASSESSMENT Chapter 26 Review/Test p. 419–420

CHECKPOINT
Chapters 25–26 Math Fun p. 421, Technology p. 422
Chapters 25–26 Take-Home Book pp. 422A–422B, Review/Test pp. 423–424
Chapters 25–26 Performance Assessment p. 425
Chapters 1–26 Cumulative Review p. 426

Chapter 27 Multiply and Divide

BIG IDEA
Multiplication names the whole when the number of equal parts is known and the number in each part is known.

PLANNING GUIDE

Introducing the Chapter p. 427   **School-Home Connection** p. 428

OBJECTIVE	VOCABULARY	RESOURCES	GEORGIA QCC OBJECTIVES
LESSON 27.1 **1 DAY** **Counting Equal Groups** pp. 429A–430A Objective To explore the concept of multiplication by making equal groups and identifying how many in all	equal groups in all	■ Problem Solving, ■ Reteach, ■ Practice, ■ Enrichment Worksheets 27.1 ● **Carnival Countdown** • *Snap Clowns*, p. 430A ▢ Transparencies Problem of the Day 27 Spiral Review 70	
LESSON 27.2 **1 DAY** **How Many in Each Group?** pp. 431A–432A Objective To explore the concept of division by making equal groups and identifying how many are in each group	equal groups	■ Problem Solving, ■ Reteach, ■ Practice, ■ Enrichment Worksheets 27.2 ● **Carnival Countdown** • *Snap Clowns*, p. 432A ▢ Transparencies Problem of the Day 27 Spiral Review 70	**QCC 1.30** Recognizes equivalent and nonequivalent sets using one-to-one correspondence. **QCC 1.36** Solves one- and two-step word problems. **QCC 1.38** Recalls addition facts and related subtraction facts presented vertically and horizontally.
LESSON 27.3 **1 DAY** **How Many Groups?** pp. 433A–434A Objective To explore the concept of division by separating a group of objects to identify how many equal groups	equal groups	■ Problem Solving, ■ Reteach, ■ Practice, ■ Enrichment Worksheets 27.3 ▢ Transparencies Problem of the Day 27 Spiral Review 71	**QCC 1.30** Recognizes equivalent and nonequivalent sets using one-to-one correspondence.
LESSON 27.4 **2 DAYS** **Problem-Solving Strategy: Draw a Picture** pp. 435A–436A Objective To use the problem-solving strategy *draw a picture* to solve problems	equal groups	■ Reading Strategy • *Use Word Clues,* ■ Reteach, ■ Practice, ■ Enrichment Worksheets 27.4 ● **Zoo Zillions** • *Fish Stories*, p. 436A Problem-Solving Think Along, TR p. R113 ▢ Transparency Spiral Review 71	**QCC 1.30** Recognizes equivalent and nonequivalent sets using one-to-one correspondence. **QCC 1.36** Solves one- and two-step word problems. **QCC 1.38** Recalls addition facts and related subtraction facts presented vertically and horizontally.

CHAPTER ASSESSMENT **Chapter 27 Review/Test p. 437–438**

Chapter 28 | Two-Digit Addition and Subtraction

BIG IDEA

Efficient computation involves understanding the connection among basic facts, properties, and place value.

PLANNING GUIDE

Introducing the Chapter p. 439   **School-Home Connection** p. 440

OBJECTIVE	VOCABULARY	RESOURCES	GEORGIA QCC OBJECTIVES
LESSON 28.1 **2 DAYS** **Adding and Subtracting Tens** pp. 441A–442A Objective To add and subtract tens	in all tens sum are left	■ Problem Solving, ■ Reteach, ■ Practice, ■ Enrichment Worksheets 28.1 🔵 **Carnival Countdown** • *Bubble Band*, p. 442A ▢ Transparencies Problem of the Day 28 Spiral Review 72	**QCC 1.39** Uses models to explore adding and subtracting two-digit numbers without regrouping. **QCC 1.40** Adds and subtracts 2-digit whole numbers without regrouping vertically and horizontally.
LESSON 28.2 **1 DAY** **Adding Tens and Ones** pp. 443A–444A Objective To add tens and ones without regrouping	ones tens	■ Problem Solving, ■ Reteach, ■ Practice, ■ Enrichment Worksheets 28.2 🔵 **Carnival Countdown** • *Giggle Factory*, p. 444A ▢ Transparencies Problem of the Day 28 Spiral Review 72	**QCC 1.39** Uses models to explore adding and subtracting two-digit numbers without regrouping. **QCC 1.40** Adds and subtracts 2-digit whole numbers without regrouping vertically and horizontally.
LESSON 28.3 **1 DAY** **Subtracting Tens and Ones** pp. 445A–446A Objective To subtract tens and ones without regrouping	equal groups	■ Problem Solving, ■ Reteach, ■ Practice, ■ Enrichment Worksheets 28.3 🔵 **Zoo Zillions** • *Annie's Jungle Trail*, p. 446A ▢ Transparencies Problem of the Day 28 Spiral Review 73	**QCC 1.39** Uses models to explore adding and subtracting two-digit numbers without regrouping. **QCC 1.40** Adds and subtracts 2-digit whole numbers without regrouping vertically and horizontally.
LESSON 28.4 **1 DAY** **Problem Solving: Logical Reasoning** pp. 447A–448A Objective To use the problem-solving strategy *use logical reasoning* to solve problems	in all are left	■ Reading Strategy • *Use Word Clues*, ■ Reteach, ■ Practice, ■ Enrichment Worksheets 28.4 Problem-Solving Think Along, TR p. R113 ▢ Transparencies Problem of the Day 28 Spiral Review 73	**QCC 1.36** Solves one- and two-step word problems. **QCC 1.38** Recalls addition facts and related subtraction facts presented vertically and horizontally.

CHAPTER ASSESSMENT   Chapter 28 Review/Test p. 449–450

CHECKPOINT
Chapters 27–28 Math Fun p. 451, Technology p. 452
Chapters 27–28 Take-Home Book pp. 452A–452B, Review/Test pp. 453–454
Chapters 27–28 Performance Assessment p. 455
Chapters 1–28 Cumulative Review p. 456

Teacher's Notes

The Tale of
Peter Rabbit

by Beatrix Potter

Illustrated by Rod Ruth

gb ® GOLDEN PRESS
Western Publishing Company, Inc.
Racine, Wisconsin

Sixth Printing, 1974

GOLDEN, A BIG GOLDEN BOOK, and GOLDEN PRESS®
are trademarks of Western Publishing Company, Inc.

ISBN 0-307-10486-9

Once upon a time there were four little rabbits, and their names were Flopsy, Mopsy, Cotton-tail, and Peter. They lived with their mother in a sandbank, underneath the root of a very big fir tree.

"Now, my dears," said old Mrs. Rabbit one morning, "you may go into the fields or down the lane, but don't go into Mr. McGregor's garden. Your father had an accident there; he was put in a pie by Mrs. McGregor. Now run along, and don't get into mischief. I am going out."

Then old Mrs. Rabbit took a basket and her umbrella and went through the wood to the baker's. She bought a loaf of brown bread and five currant buns.

Flopsy, Mopsy, and Cotton-tail, who were good little bunnies, went down the lane to gather blackberries.

But Peter, who was very naughty, ran straight away to Mr. McGregor's garden and squeezed under the gate!

First he ate some lettuce

and some French beans,

and then he ate
some radishes.
And then, feeling
rather sick, he
went to look for
some parsley.

But round the end of a cucumber frame, whom should he meet but Mr. McGregor!

Mr. McGregor was on his hands and knees planting out young cabbages, but he jumped up and ran after Peter, waving a rake and calling out, "Stop, thief!"

Peter was most dreadfully frightened. He rushed all over the garden, for he had forgotten the way back to the gate. He lost one of his shoes among the cabbages, and the other shoe amongst the potatoes.

After losing them, he ran on four legs and went faster, so that I think he might have got away altogether if he had not unfortunately run into a gooseberry net and got caught by the large buttons on his jacket. It was a blue jacket with brass buttons, quite new.

Peter gave himself up for lost and shed big tears. But his sobs were overheard by some friendly sparrows, who flew to him in great excitement and implored him to exert himself.

Mr. McGregor came up with a sieve, which he intended to pop upon the top of Peter. But Peter wriggled out just in time, leaving his jacket behind him —

and rushed into the tool shed
and jumped into a can.

It would have been
a beautiful thing to
hide in,

if it had not had so much water in it.

Mr. McGregor was quite sure that Peter was somewhere in the tool shed, perhaps hidden underneath a flower pot. He began to turn them over carefully, looking under each.

Presently Peter sneezed — "Kertyschoo!"

Mr. McGregor was after him in no time and tried to put his foot upon Peter, who jumped out of a window, upsetting three plants. The window was too small for Mr. McGregor, and he was tired of running after Peter. He went back to his work.

Peter sat down to rest. He was out of breath and trembling with fright, and he had not the least idea which way to go. Also, he was very damp with sitting in that can.

After a time he began to wander about, going lippity — lippity — not very fast, and looking around.

He found a door in a wall, but it was locked, and there was no room for a fat little rabbit to squeeze underneath.

An old mouse was running in and out over the stone doorstep, carrying peas and beans to her family in the wood. Peter asked her the way to the gate, but she had such a large pea in her mouth that she could not answer. She only shook her head at him. Peter began to cry.

Then he tried to find his way straight across the garden, but he became more and more puzzled. Presently, he came to a pond where Mr. McGregor filled his water cans. A white cat was staring at some goldfish; she sat very, very still, but now and then the tip of her tail twitched as if it were alive. Peter thought it best to go away without speaking to her; he had heard about cats from his cousin, little Benjamin Bunny.

He went back
towards the tool shed,

but suddenly, quite close
to him, he heard the noise
of a hoe — scr-r-ritch, scratch,
scratch, scritch.

Peter scuttered underneath the bushes. But presently, as nothing happened, he came out and climbed upon a wheelbarrow and peeped over. The first thing he saw was Mr. McGregor hoeing onions. His back was turned towards Peter, and beyond him was the gate!

Peter got down very quietly off the wheelbarrow and started running as fast as he could go along a straight walk behind some black-currant bushes.

Mr. McGregor caught sight of him at the corner, but Peter did not care. He slipped underneath the gate and was safe at last in the wood outside the garden.

Mr. McGregor hung up the little jacket and the shoes for a scarecrow to frighten the blackbirds.

Peter never stopped running or looked behind him till he got home to the big fir tree. He was so tired that he flopped down upon the nice soft sand on the floor of the rabbit hole and shut his eyes. His mother was busy cooking; she wondered what he had done with his clothes. It was the second little jacket and pair of shoes that Peter had lost in a fortnight!

I am sorry to say that Peter was not very well during the evening. His mother put him to bed and made some camomile tea, and she gave a dose of it to Peter!

"One tablespoonful to be taken at bedtime."

But Flopsy, Mopsy, and Cotton-tail had bread and milk and blackberries for supper.